Summer

Winter

This  Annual belongs to

....

Age

....

Come and guess with Jess!

?

ANNUAL 2012

EGMONT
We bring stories to life

First published in Great Britain 2011
by Egmont UK Limited
239 Kensington High Street, London W8 6SA

Editor: Laura Green. Designer: Jo Bestall.

Guess with Jess®: © 2011 Woodland Animations Limited,
a division of Classic Media UK Limited. All rights reserved.

ISBN 978 1 4052 5814 2
1 3 5 7 9 10 8 6 4 2
Printed in Italy

All rights reserved. No part of this publication may be reproduced,
stored in a retrieval system, or transmitted in any form or by any means, electronic, mechanical,
photocopying, recording or otherwise, without the prior permission of the publisher and copyright owner.

Adult supervision is recommended when glue, paint, scissors and other sharp points are in use.

Contents

Welcome 7
Meet the gang! 8

It's Spring! 10
Let's draw! 11
Story: What's your favourite thing about spring? 12
Where's the rainbow? 18
What's on your kite? 19
Can you rescue Billie? 20
Guess with Jess 22
Spash and spell 23

It's Summer! 24
Story: Where have all the stars gone? 26
Star light! 32
Guess with Jess 34
Flower power! 35
What can you find in Horace's pond? 36

It's Autumn! 38
Pattern match 39
Story: How can the gang keep warm in autumn? 40
Can you dance? 46
Guess with Jess 47
Let's make a tree! 48
Who can fly the highest? 50

It's Winter! 52
Hide-and-seek 53
Story: Why are there so many ladybirds in the barn? 54
Can you make a ladybird? 60
Colouring fun! 61
Can you find the way home? 62
Let's go inside! 64
Guess with Jess 65

My season wheel 66
Answers 68

Hey, everyone!

Welcome to Greendale Farm! I'm Jess and I can't wait to show you around my home. You can meet my friends, play some games and help me find answers to some BIG questions!

You can find all the answers on page 68.

Come on then ... let's go!

Jess

Yippety yay, hurray!

Meet the gang!

Jess lives in this red barn. He is full of energy and he loves finding answers to BIG questions! **Where do you live?**

Jinx and Joey are roly-poly puppies! They love to play Tail Chase around the Twisty Tree. **What's your favourite game?**

Willow lives in the stable. She is wise and always helps the gang with their questions. **Who can you help today?**

It's spring!

Mimi has made a list of things you see in the spring. Can you find them in the big picture? Circle each object as you spot it.

1 butterfly   2 birds   3 blossom flowers

What else you can find in spring? Here's a clue – they grow in the ground and are very colourful. Look at the picture to find the answer!

What's your favourite thing about spring?

It was the first day of spring on Greendale Farm. Jess had just woken up in his barn.

"Ah, the birds are singing," said Jess, peeping out from his blanket.

Jess raced outside to listen to the birdsong.

"Tweet! Tweet! Tweet!" they sang.

"Oh, I love spring!" smiled Jess. "I wonder if everyone else likes spring, too. Come on, let's find out!"

Mimi was busy watering the flowers in her garden.

Hey, Mimi! What do you love most about spring?

"I love the daffodils," said Mimi.

"Me too!" said Jess. "And the fresh leaves, and the singing birds."

"But what's your favourite thing?" asked Mimi. Jess thought for second …

"Hey! That's the big question! What's my favourite thing about spring?"

Atishoo!

Jess went to find Willow.

"Well, my favourite thing about spring is the blossom," said Willow.

But the blossom made Jess sneezy. Blossom definitely wasn't Jess' favourite thing.

Maybe Horace could help Jess find the answer.

Next stop was Baa and Billie's paddock.

"I love all the new flowers that grow in the meadow," said Billie, inspecting a flower with her magnifying glass.

"And this new spring grass tastes delicious!" said Baa.

Jess liked the new flowers and he liked the grass, but they weren't his favourite things.

Just then the little bird appeared again.

Tweet! Tweet! Tweet!

Let's follow her!

"Maybe she can help me find the answer!" said Jess, bounding after the singing bird.

Jess, Billie and Baa followed the bird past Horace's pond, over the meadow, through the Whispering Wood and soon, they were back at Jess' barn.

"Look, she's flown into those leaves!" cried Billie, pointing to a tree.

There, tucked away in the branches, was a nest of baby birds!

Tweet! Tweet! Tweet!

"Spring babies!" said Jess. "They're so cute!"

Yippety yay! Hurray!

Then Jess had a thought.

"That's it! Baby birds! They're my favourite thing about spring," said Jess. "I found the answer!"

Where's the rainbow?

Guide Baa through the maze to the rainbow. Pick up each colour of the rainbow on your way. Shout the colours out loud as you pass them! Use the colour key at the bottom of the page if you need help.

start

finish

What's your favourite colour?

 red
 orange
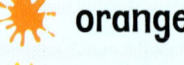 yellow
 green

 blue
 indigo
 violet

What's on your kite?

It's a breezy afternoon and the gang are flying kites in the sky.

Design your own kite so you can join the fun!

Have you ever flown a kite?

Can you rescue Billie?

Billie needs Jess' help – and fast! He's stuck up a tree and can't get down. But there are lots of things in Jess' way. Guide Jess through the farm, copying the actions to help him through the obstacles along the way!

Start

1. Uh oh! Mimi has spilt paint! Bounce like a rabbit over the mess!

2. Can you leap like a frog to get over the hay bales?

3. Can you crawl on the floor to get through the hollow log?

Guess with Jess

Jess has a BIG question!

What makes a TWIT TWOO noise?

Can you guess?

Here's a clue ... It comes out at night!

Choose a card then turn to page 68 to find the answer!

1. a ladybird

2. a bee

3. an owl

"I guessed with Jess!"
Colour in the rosette when you've found the answer!

Splash and spell

There's a spring shower and Jinx and Joey are playing in the puddles! SPLASH! Trace over these words all about water. Start each letter at the blue raindrop.

bath

sea

rain

splash

It's summer!

The sun is hot and the bees are buzzing.
It's time for a summer party – yippee!

1

These party pictures look the same, but there are 6 differences in picture 2. Can you spot them all? Colour in a sun as you find each one.

What colour is the sunshine?

Where have all the stars gone?

It was a hot summer's night. Jess, Jinx and Joey were having a sleepover in Jess' barn.

It was warm inside the barn, so the friends went outside to cool down. The sky was filled with twinkling stars!

"They're so pretty," said Jess. "Willow says you can wish on stars."

Ooh, what are you going to wish for, Jess?

Jess thought for a moment, then suddenly, he felt very sleepy indeed.

"I'll make my wish in the morning ..." Jess yawned, as he climbed into his basket.

The pups climbed into their beds too, and soon everyone was fast asleep.

ZZZzz!

The next morning, Jess woke up bright and early.

"Wake up, pups! I've thought of a wish for the stars!

"Star light, star bright, make my wish come true tonight. I wish I could have an adventure!" said Jess.

But when the friends ran outside, the sun was shining brightly and there were no stars in the sky.

"How are you going to make a wish if they are no stars?" asked Joey, rubbing his eyes.

Jess looked up at the blue sky. Then he had a thought ...

"Hey! That's the big question! Where have all the stars gone"

Jess ran over to the paddock. He told Baa and Billie about the stars.

"They must be hiding," said Billie. "I know! Let's go on a star hunt!"

The friends jumped up in excitement and ran off to search for the missing stars.

"Then Jess can make a wish on his own stars!"

Over in Mimi's hutch, the pups were busy with their own plan. They had found some silver foil and were making some sparkly stars for Jess!

At the meadow, Jess, Baa and Billie were getting tired. They had looked all over the farm for the stars and the sun was very hot.

Suddenly Billie jumped up. "Look!" she cried. "Stars!"

Sure enough, the field ahead was filled with twinkling lights.

"Stars! They must have fallen from the sky!" said Jess. "Now I can make my wish ..."

"Wait!" said Billie, inspecting the lights with her magnifying glass. "They're not stars after all. They're dew drops!"

Oh dear. Jess felt very disappointed. Where could the stars be hiding?

Over at Mimi's hutch, Jinx was shining a light at the foil stars. They were very twinkly!

Then she heard somebody at the door. It was Jess and Mimi!

The pups turned off the torch and hid behind the plant pots.

Jess and Mimi saw the foil stars twinkling in the light.

"My stars!" Jess gasped. "I've found my stars ..."

Then they heard a loud

CRASH ...!

It was Jinx and Joey. They had tumbled over the plant pots!

"Oh, they're not real stars," said Joey. "We made them so you could make a wish!"

We're sorry, Jess!

Jess took one of the stars outside. It didn't look as twinkly as it had in the dark. Jess had a thought ...

"Hey! When did we first see the stars?" asked Jess. "At night! I think the stars have been in the sky the whole time!"

Everybody was confused.

"The stars don't go away," said Jess. "The sun shines brighter than them in the daytime so we can't see them. When the sun goes to bed, we see them again. Look – everyone, watch the sky …"

As the bright sun dipped behind the hills and the sky turned dark, millions of shining stars twinkled in the sky!

Everyone gasped.

"Yippee! We found the answer!" said Jess. "Now I can make a wish on a star every night."

The stars are back!

Yippety yay! Hurray!

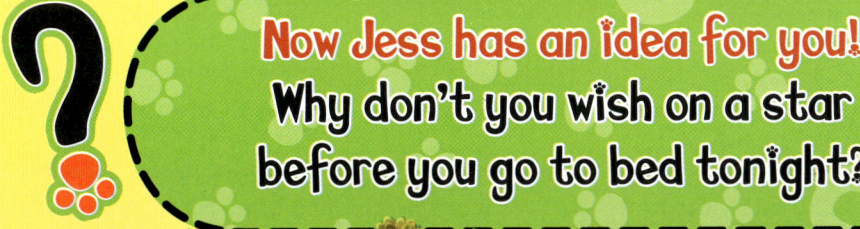

Now Jess has an idea for you! Why don't you wish on a star before you go to bed tonight?

Star light!

Now you can make your own stars! Just follow the instructions to create a night sky on your bedroom wall.

You will need:
- scissors
- sticky tape
- small torch

1 Ask an adult to photocopy this page and then help you cut around the grey shapes. Carefully cut out the star and moon shapes. Cut along the blue lines to reach your shapes.

2 Use your sticky tape to stick the blue lines back together, so the torch light won't shine through these lines.

3 Fold the tabs down along the dotted lines and stick these to the outside of the torch, with the grey shape over the glass.

4 Now for the exciting part! Wait until it gets dark outside and close your curtains. Shine the torch at your bedroom wall to create your own night sky!

There are three different star and moon shapes to choose from. Try one at a time!

Guess with Jess

Jess has a BIG question!

"How can Horace find shade from the hot sun?"

Can you guess?

Here's a clue ... It covers his head!

Choose a card then turn to page 68 to find the answer!

1 — under an umbrella

2 — on a lilypad

3 — in a meadow

"I guessed with Jess!"
Colour in the rosette when you've found the answer!

What can you find in Horace's pond?

Lots of creatures have come down to Horace's pond to keep cool. Can you find them all? Circle the creatures as you spot them, then answer Jess' questions!

Pattern match!

Look at the patterns under Billie's magnifying glass. Which close-up belongs to which creature? Take a guess then draw lines to match them up!

1.
2.
3.
4.

snail

bird

owl

fish

How can the gang keep warm in autumn?

It was a breezy morning. That afternoon, the gang were going to Willow's apple-picking party. Every autumn, the friends collected apples to make pies!

But it was cold outside. Jess couldn't keep warm.

Mimi was cold, too. "Look, all the leaves are blowing in the wind!" she said.

"Are you coming to the apple-picking party later?" asked Baa. Mimi wasn't sure. She wanted to go but she wanted to stay warm, too.

Jess had a thought ...

Brrrr!

"Hey! That's the big question! How can we all keep warm at Willow's apple-picking party?"

"That's an easy question!" said Baa. "Because I'm not cold at all."

"That's because you're covered in wool, Baa," said Jess.

"And heat leaves your body through the top of you head, so your hat is keeping you warm," added Billie.

I'm toasty and warm!

Hey, it is really warm in here!

Mimi pulled Baa's hat on her head. Maybe wearing a hat would keep the gang warm!

But there was only one woolly hat, and Jess needed to find a way to keep the whole gang warm.

Jess set off to find Horace. He might know the answer!

At the Lily Pond, Horace was hiding deep in the mud.

"Hey, Jess! This is how I stay warm when it's cold. I just bury myself in mud," said Horace. "It's like a big sloppy blanket!"

"That's given me an idea," said Jess. "Thanks, Horace!"

41

Jess raced back to Mimi's hutch.

"I know how to keep warm outside!" said Jess. "We need to cover ourselves with mud."

"Let's test it!" said the pups.

The pups dived into the slimy mud, splashing it everywhere.

Mimi wasn't so happy about Jess' idea.

"I'm a clean pink rabbit and I'm not getting dirty," she said.

"Hmm, maybe the mud only works on frogs," Jess thought.

"Nearly time for the apple-picking party!" Baa said, happily.

Oh dear. Jess was running out of time and he still hadn't found a way to keep warm at the party.

We're not feeling any warmer, Jess!

Jess set off to look for more clues. There must be something on the farm to keep all of the friends warm. Then Jess remembered what kept him cosy in his barn – straw!

Jess, Baa, Jinx, Joey and Mimi dived into a huge pile of straw.

"Ooh, snuggly!"

"Warm as toast!"

"Hmmmm!"

The gang were warm and happy in the straw, but they couldn't take the straw to the orchard for the party. Or could they?

With Mimi's help, Jess made some little coats from the straw.

"I'm so warm!" said Jinx.

The friends ran over to the orchard, to show Willow their straw coats.

43

"Look, Willow!" said Jess. "We were trying to find a way to keep warm outside and we've found the answer."

Just then, a strong breeze swept through the farm. It blew all the straw away. The friends were cold again.

"Oh dear," said Willow. "I know, let's play a game of 'Willow Says ...'"

"But we're soooo chilly!" said Jess.

"Give it a try," said Willow. "Willow says, 'run to your nearest apple and kick it around a tree!'"

Come on! Get moving, everyone!

This is fun!

The friends raced towards the apple trees.

After kicking the apples, Willow asked the friends to fetch as many apples as they could in five minutes, and then they had a race!

Jess stopped for a moment. "Hey, wait a minute. I'm toasty warm!"

"You're warm because you are running about," smiled Willow. "Running makes you warm on the inside …"

"And that makes you warm on the outside …" said Jess. "That's it! We've found the answer!"

We can all keep warm by running about!

Yippety yay! Hurray!

The friends jumped around so much, soon they were all too warm!

"Now we need to find a way to cool down for the party," said Baa.

"Let's save that question for another day," smiled Willow.

Now Jess has an idea for you!
Next time you're cold outside, why don't you run around and play games, too?

45

Can you dance?

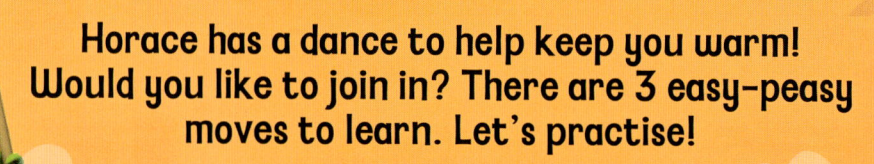

Horace has a dance to help keep you warm! Would you like to join in? There are 3 easy-peasy moves to learn. Let's practise!

1 Jump like Horace!

Jump! Jump! Jump!

2 Stamp your feet like Baa!

Stomp! Stomp! Stomp!

3 Clap your hands like Jinx!

Clap! Clap! Clap!

Now it's time to turn your moves into a real dance! Get ready … dance!

Jump → Clap → Jump → Clap → Jump

Stomp → Stomp → Clap → Clap

Jump → Jump → Clap → Stomp

Stomp → Clap → Jump

Guess with Jess

Jess has a BIG question!

What falls from trees in autumn?

Can you guess?

Here's a clue ... They turn brown!

Choose a card then turn to page 68 to find the answer!

1. sunflowers
2. birds
3. leaves

"I guessed with Jess!"
Colour in the rosette when you've found the answer!

Let's make a tree!

You will need:
A brown wax crayon
White paper
Glue
Scissors
Lots of leaves!

Look! Jess has made an autumn tree. Just follow the easy-peasy instructions to make your own tree!

1 Grab your paper and a crayon and go outside! Find a tree and place your paper over the bark. Rub your crayon over the paper, like Jess is doing. Soon you'll get a tree-bark pattern.

48

2

Collect lots of leaves! Try to pick leaves of different colours and shapes.

3

Trace over or ask an adult to photocopy this trunk shape. Then ask an adult to cut out your trunk shape and draw around it onto your tree-bark paper. Cut out your trunk and stick it on a new piece of paper.

4

Now it's time to stick your leaves on. Use as many leaves as you can so your tree is bursting with colour!

? Can you think of 5 different words about trees?

Who can fly the highest?

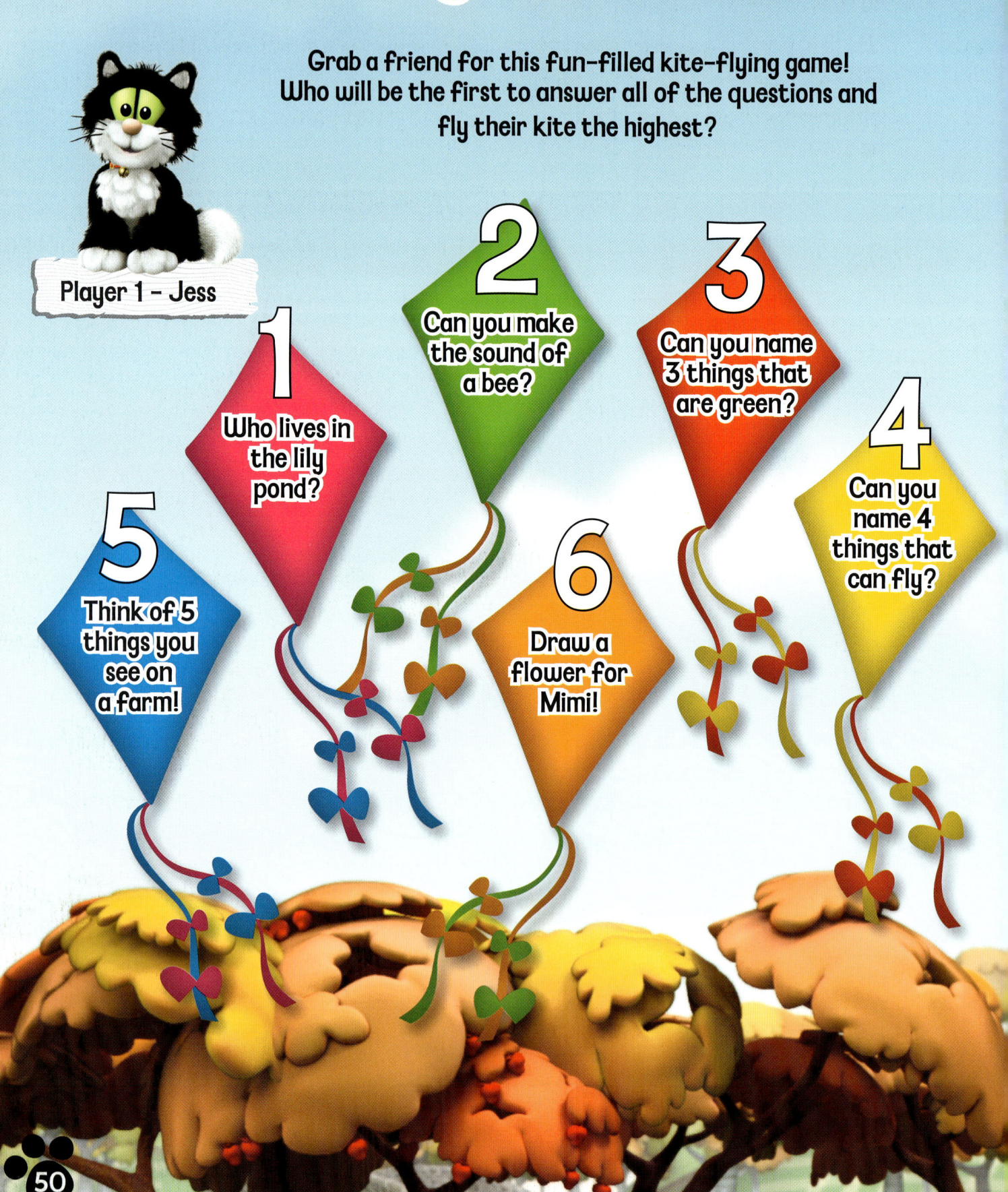

Grab a friend for this fun-filled kite-flying game! Who will be the first to answer all of the questions and fly their kite the highest?

Player 1 - Jess

1 Who lives in the lily pond?

2 Can you make the sound of a bee?

3 Can you name 3 things that are green?

4 Can you name 4 things that can fly?

5 Think of 5 things you see on a farm!

6 Draw a flower for Mimi!

How to play:

- You need a dice and two players
- Both pages have the same challenges, but one player follows Jess' kites and one player follows Horace's kites
- Take it in turns to throw the dice and then do the challenge on the kite with the same number as the dice
- Colour in the number on the kite once you've completed the challenge. The first to complete all six is the winner!

Player 2 - Horace

1 Who lives in the lily pond?

2 Can you make the sound of a bee?

3 Can you name 3 things that are green?

4 Can you name 4 things that can fly?

5 Think of 5 things you see on a farm!

6 Draw a flower for Mimi!

It's winter!

It's winter time! Greendale Farm has turned icy and cold. Icicles have frozen over these photographs of Jess and the gang.
Can you tell which friend is in each photograph?

1

2

3

4

Hide-and-seek

Jess, Billie, Jinx and Mimi are playing hide-and-seek. Can you spot them all? Shout their names out loud each time you spot a friend!

Why are there so many ladybirds in the barn?

"Brr... it's cold today!"

It was a cold, wintry morning on the farm. The ground was frosty and there were icicles hanging from the trees.

Jess was cuddled up inside his barn, keeping warm.

Suddenly, the door to the barn crashed open.

It was Jinx and Joey!

"Guess what, Jess? Willow's having a winter party, with games and everything!"

Just then, a little ladybird flew up and landed right on Jess' nose!

"A ladybird!" giggled Jinx. "She's so pretty."

"Oh, hello ladybird!"

"There's one over here, too!" said Joey, running over to the window.

"And there's another one!" said Jinx, pointing to the floor.

"Look! They're everywhere!" cried Joey.

Sure enough, there were ladybirds on the floor, on the hay bales and even in Jess' basket!

Jess was sure that the ladybirds weren't there yesterday.

Suddenly, Jess had a thought …

"Hey! That's the big question! Why are there so many ladybirds in my barn?"

Jess ran over to Mimi's hutch to see if he could spot any ladybirds in her garden.

Mimi was busy sorting through a big pile of carrots.

"You must be hungry!" said Jess.

Mimi laughed. "I'm not eating them all at once, silly! Carrots don't grow all year round so I have to save them."

You're so clever, Mimi!

"Maybe you can help me with my big question about ladybirds," said Jess. "I'm trying to find out why there are so many in my barn."

"They might be looking for greenfly," said Mimi. "But I'm not sure. Why don't you ask Billie? She's always looking at bugs."

"Great idea!" said Jess, running out of the door. "Thanks, Mimi!"

When Jess arrived at the paddock, Baa and Billie were talking to a bird.

"See you again, little bird," said Billie. "Have a safe trip!"

"What's happening?" Jess asked, puzzled.

"Now it's winter, it's too cold for her here," said Baa.

"Goodbye, birdie!"

"She's flying away to a warmer country with her friends," added Billie.

"That's it!" said Jess. "The ladybirds must meet up to fly to a warmer country, too!"

But when Jess got back to his barn, it didn't look like the ladybirds were going to fly away anywhere.

They were all fast asleep in the hay.

Jinx and Joey bounced back into the barn to find Jess.

"Come on, Jess!" said Joey. "It's time for the winter party …"

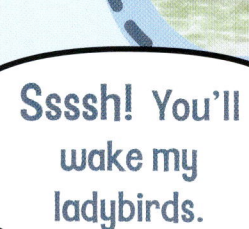

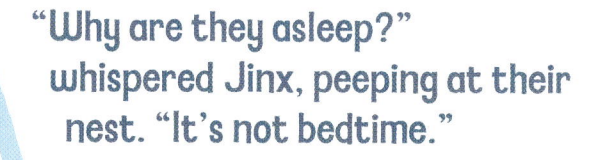

Ssssh! You'll wake my ladybirds.

"Why are they asleep?" whispered Jinx, peeping at their nest. "It's not bedtime."

"That's what I'm trying to find out," said Jess. "Let's find Willow. She'll know the answer!"

When the friends arrived at the stable, Willow was peering into a bush.

"Come and look at this," she whispered to the friends. "But you must be very, very quiet."

There, tucked up inside the bush, was a sleeping hedgehog!

"He's going to be asleep for the whole of winter," said Willow. "Some animals find life hard in the cold weather, so they eat as much as they can and then find somewhere warm to sleep until winter is over. It's called hibernation."

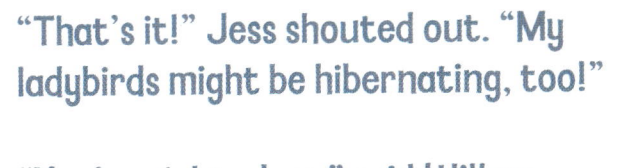

"That's it!" Jess shouted out. "My ladybirds might be hibernating, too!"

"You're right, Jess," said Willow. "Ladybirds do hibernate. They'll sleep up until spring time."

"Yippee! We found the answer!" said Jess. "Now we can party!"

Yippety yay! Hurray!

Now Jess has an idea for you!
"When it's winter, why don't you look out for sleeping ladybirds or hedgehogs? Just be careful not to wake them up!"

Can you make a ladybird?

Follow these instructions to make your own ladybird.

You will need:
red card
black pipe cleaners
scissors
white paper
black felt tip
glue

Step 1
Ask an adult to cut out the oval body and two wings from the red card.

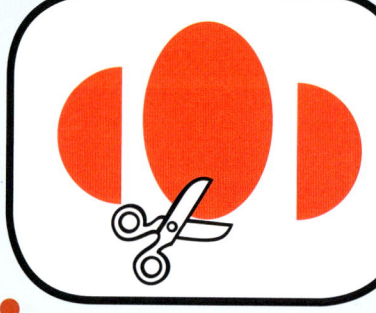

Step 2
Draw small black dots on the wings with your pen.

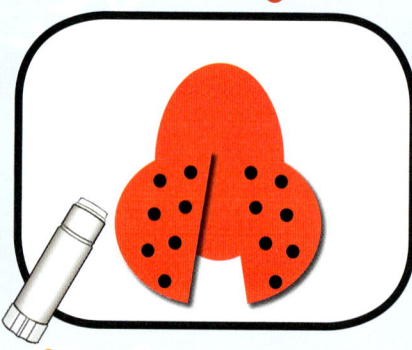

Step 3
Stick the wings onto the body.

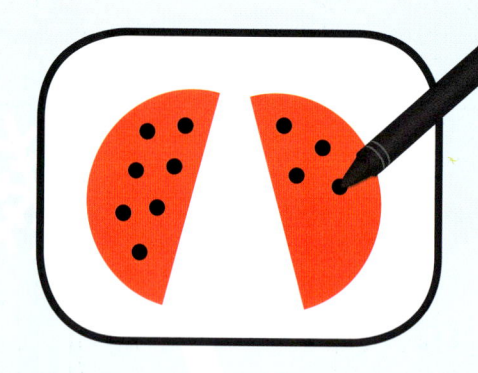

Step 4
Cut out 2 white circles for the eyes and draw black dots on them. Fold the ends of your pipe cleaners over and wrap them around the stem. Stick the pipe cleaner legs under the body.

When you've finished, make a nest out of cotton wool so your ladybird can hibernate!

Do you remember what hibernate means? Go back to the story to find out!

60

Colouring fun!

Fill the picture with lots of colour. Then add some snowflakes, and a snowman!

Can you find the way home?

The snow has turned into a blizzard and Jess and the gang can't find their way home! Use your finger to guide Jess through the snowy maze to his barn, finding his friends along the way.

Each time you rescue a friend, tick a box below.

start →

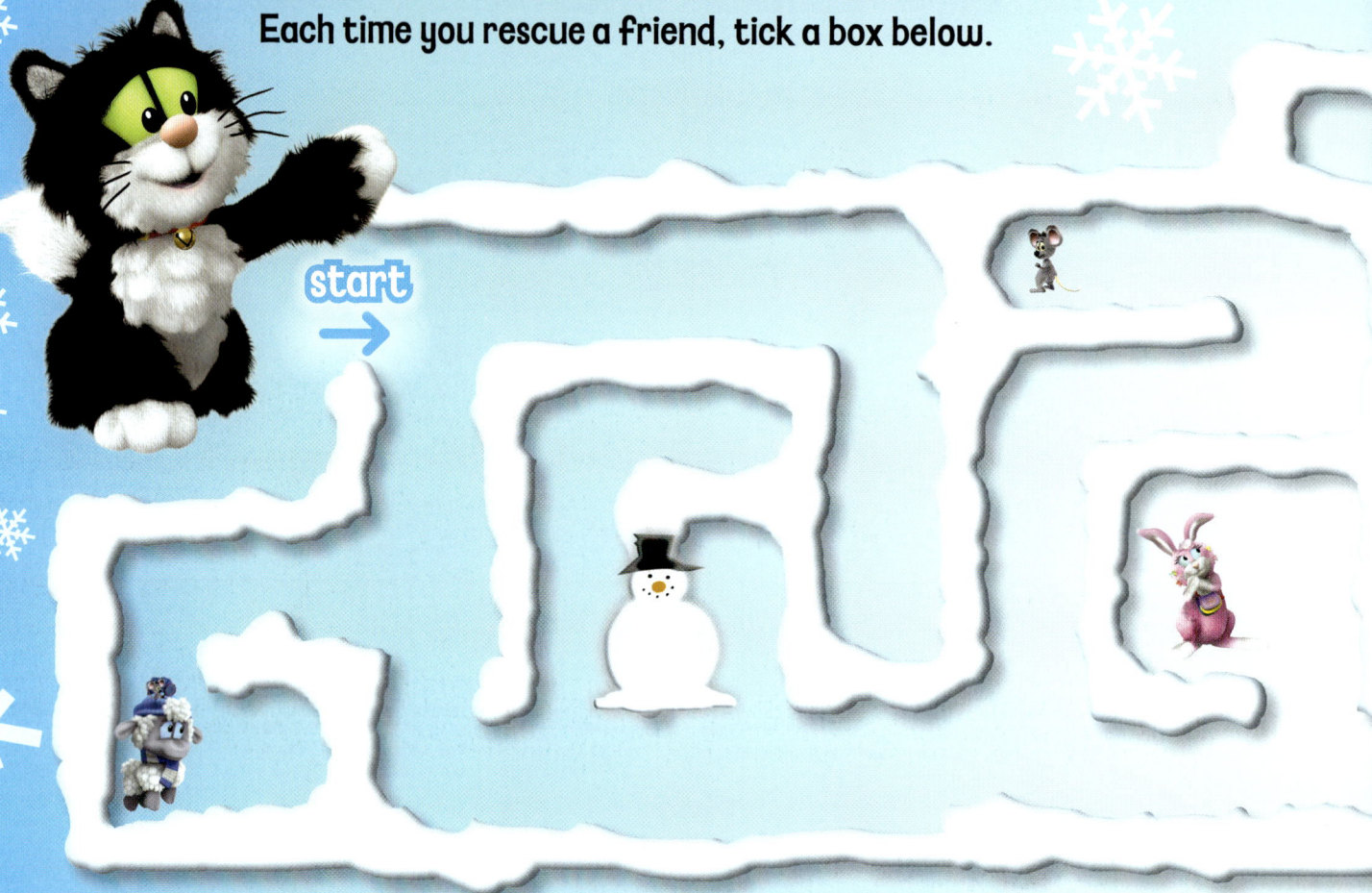

I have rescued:

Baa ☐   Billie ☐   Mimi ☐

finish

Hurray! We've made it!

Joey   Jinx   Horace

Let's go inside!

Using the big square as a starting point, draw the best home you can imagine so you have somewhere to keep cosy!

What colour is your home?

Guess with Jess

Jess has a BIG question!

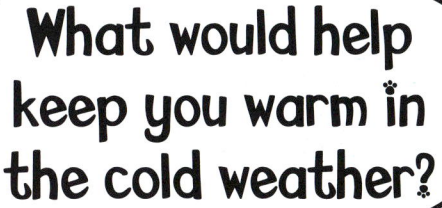

What would help keep you warm in the cold weather?

Can you guess?

Here's a clue ... It's fluffy!

Choose a card then turn to page 68 to find the answer!

1. a scarf
2. a worm
3. a basket

"I guessed with Jess!"
Colour in the rosette when you've found the answer!

My season wheel

Winter

Spring

Autumn

Summer

What is your favourite season?

Hey! It's me, Jess.

Now you've spent a whole year in Greendale, can you help me find answers to these questions about seasons? Use your season wheel to find the answers!

1. In what season can you find icicles hanging from the roof?

2. When is the sun hot, hot, hot?

3. When do the leaves turn brown and fall from the trees?

4. When do the first flowers of the year start to bloom?

Hurray! You guessed with me! Yippee!

It's time to go now. But remember to watch out for all the amazing things that happen in spring, summer, autumn and winter around you!

Come and see us again soon!

Jess

Answers!

page 10:

page 36:

page 38: Jess collects 3 apples, Mimi collects 4 apples and Baa collects 5 apples.

page 39: 1) bird, 2) owl, 3) fish, 4) snail

page 47: 3) leaves

page 52: 1) Willow, 2) Baa, 3) Billie, 4) Joey

page 53:

page 18:

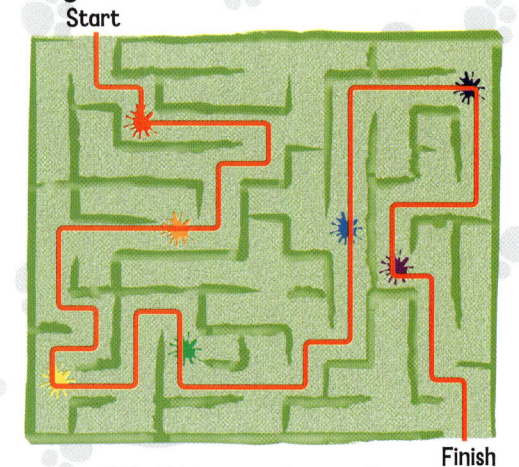

page 22: 3) an owl

page 25:

page 62:

page 34: 1) under an umbrella

page 35: path 2

page 65: 1) a scarf

Spring

Autumn